A
Beauty
Has
Come

A Beauty Has Come

Jasmine Gibson

Nightboat Books
New York

ISBN: 978-1-643-62175-3

Cover design by Megan Tatem and Kit Schluter
Design and typesetting by HR Hegnauer
Typeset in Adobe Garamond Pro and Baker Signet BT

Cataloging-in-publication data is available from the Library of Congress

Nightboat Books
New York
www.nightboat.org

Eternity is not of this world, but man will outlive classes and will continue to produce and make history, since he can never free himself from the burden of his needs, both of mind and of body, which are the basis of the development of the forces of production.

—Amilcar Cabral, "The Weapon Of Theory"

Always and forever, near or far
Safe in your bosom here we are
Pain does not mean feel no joy
—Bad Brains, "Re-Ignition"

A hundred black faces turned round in their rows to peer; and beyond, a black Angel of Doom was beating a book in a pulpit. It was a negro church; and the preacher's text was about the blackness of darkness, and the weeping and wailing and teeth-gnashing there.

—Herman Melville, *Moby Dick, Or the Whale*

Among all the things you could be by now if Sigmund Freud's wife were your mother is someone who understands the dozens, the intricate verboseness of America's inner city.

—Dr. Hortense J. Spillers, "'All the Things You Could Be by Now If Sigmund Freud's Wife Was Your Mother': Psychoanalysis and Race"

Table of Contents

Glyph

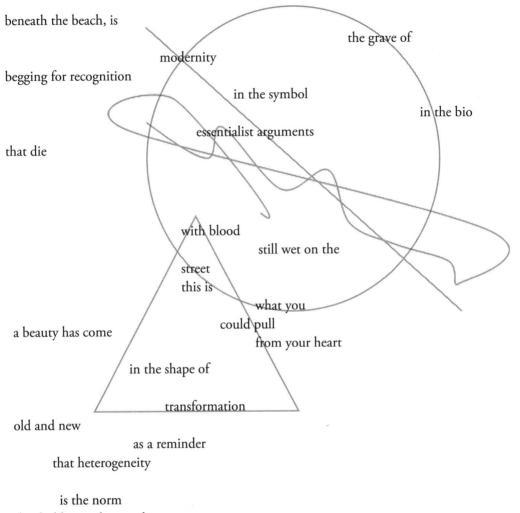

beneath the beach, is

the grave of

modernity

begging for recognition

in the symbol

in the bio

essentialist arguments

that die

with blood

still wet on the

street

this is

what you

could pull

from your heart

a beauty has come

in the shape of

transformation

old and new

as a reminder

that heterogeneity

is the norm

that holds too close to the concept

of standing still

there is also resistance

THE
BEAUTIFUL
ONE HAS
COME

Nefertiti, The Beautiful One Has Come

Come into the Black
                    Turn to Blue

Leave burdened for the dawn
Leave sore from muscles'   intricate movements   days past
When did the tongue ever utter a sound against the

hallow Tao?   Moving with it

            the goddesses and demons that guard each movement   I am in
        in reproach

   In between
                Betwixt
                    Moving with vowels

consonants   definitions of encephalopathy

                                Grey matter as holding space for
                                political struggle against biological
                                determinism
                                The unconscious is real:

1. The embodiment of self and self within others experiential discharge. Oneiroi.
    These pleasures come twinned.

2. From the slip of my nasal cavity, to the slip of the rays within a band of dust, this circlet takes the tongue.
   If you see your inner child on the road, feed them

3. Within the haze, within the room, the Blackness of Darkness is staged: Whale enters Jonah, Jonah enters Bartleby. Who has time to bear the guise of a saint, when it is man that makes indecisive images.

Marble marred by bullet holes   where runoff time is laid   The beautiful one has come
to the valley   Alte   Neue   Alte   past misgivings   It should be considered ill fated to

        be worshiped by banal evil

The beautiful one has come   To the valley   Between two rivers   veiled forest
        whooshing stumbling   Birl swamp

  Enter

        I

                    Enter

Historical monolith

                                                        A Beauty Has Come

along with the topography of deserts
and promises of frankincense and milk

Let   arrows
                            rain from
                                        Robbie Shakespeare's bass guitar
Your private life is wearing me out

Resist document

                        A Beauty Has Come

Put di spotlight pon di devils   And see their luminescent wings glow under

        a neon

        moon

3

Only Shallow

I watch whole intestines spill forth
into the Martin Luther King Booty Bounce Weekend
the steady climb of bass lures me into auditory trance
moving within the errors of
the numbering of days and frustration of regime change
we collapse as limbs exalt toward
futurity rather towards a milquetoast gaze
I've made myself twice the bastard
seeking my own vision
preparing for impending darkness after a few weeks of artificial light
amid the beach, there is the shape of
Brooklyn as Disneyland enclosed within the nights
of wet pussy in my mouth in a basement bathroom
to the song of someone's life partner explaining that
love is not a fence but a meadow
Have you heard the echo of what happened?
Have you fallen into the feedback loop that
has come to be realized
The past four years split into two
one a meditation on the passing glances of betrayal
and the second
love welcoming me
as John the Virgin holds onto me
within this picture
you can tell the faint stillness
of change pushing through my veil

as fungible as the next stand in

      for poetry

                           doing

                      the lord's

                      work

     at another turn of absolution at the end of the world

death erases past trespasses

and other orating to their god

about how all sacrifices must be atoned for

How High the Moon

The ache of debris settling against teeth
I am awake and we are all
going to work in some way or another
I love   love
I love vengeance and know the limits of said love
there is someone on
someone's second cousin
thrice removed via the management of bonds
whether desire lies within the presented vessel
an animated machine of desire
a metropolis amongst multiple origin stories
This is all dull and unimportant to internationalist politics

It is winter
and I am celebrating love
I am amongst others celebrating the nation
we stumble and shuffle upon the graves of others
and I feel the German psych rock coming on as an apology
celebrating ethnonationalism over breakfast
so many people died during good weather
bad weather while *j a z z z z z z z z z z z* played
while Sarah Vaughan sung to moon
we are hung
collapsed in time

shooobedopeedoozeeebewweeeeeet
hhhhheeemooooon

doesn't care when there is ash to be accounted for

there'd be places that would calmly

invite a continuation of the same regime

this time PG rated for state mandated and approved family structures

Lou Bond's "To The Establishment"

All my of my past love lives disappeared
under the great wool of
a burdened season
beloved affinity for machinery
making carceral aliens with steel lined veins

Feel me out
let me know my consumption patterns are what got me to this place

How I am to compete with the dead
when all you want to do
while I'm alive
is bleed for you
on a mountain top
orating
how you can "get your life"
in a five-line stanza

Coming up with a tone
that echoes all former love and
work obligations

Sis you ok?

                                          Sis you alright???

Sis

S
is
sississi
ssissss
ssssssss
ssssssss
ssssssss
ssss
s

SSSSSSSSSS

SSSSSSSSSS

SSSSiiiiiiiii

i

iiiiiiiiiissssssssssssssssssssssssssssssssssssssssssssssssssssssssssssssssssssssssssssssssssssssssssssssssssss

sssssssssssssssss

Isisisis

Is it alright?

cried from the belly from an infernal night
I'm calling you to fly out
I'm calling you to make an advance directive
enough friends have died in fires and car accidents
I just wanted a

girlgirl
girlgurli
nmyhead

to be alive and possibly
live long enough to develop an overgrowth over future possibilities
we're always checking your skin in bed
I'm saying squeeze my cyst till I'm empty
You're planning reactions to your parent's death
I'm making plans for childhood homes

Allowing myself the deliciousness of impossibilities

Waged Beginnings

Changing with the
waxing phases of Pluto
bodies bend to
the alphabet letters on the fridge
blood to
sell
cell to
Blood

Bone meets me here
stone meets me where
I cannot see you seeing   me in the flesh upon stone
upon   you
I cannot count the last time
I embodied this   dexterity
                        stone meets fat meets years of waste
laboring time
and how I've had nothing
but time to seam myself
into the hem of this historical moment

When the moon changes
I bleed into the office walls of appreciation
unequal pleasures beget unequal wages

Clothesline

The transitional phenomena represent the early stages of the use of illusion, without which there is no meaning for the human being in the idea of a relationship with an object that is perceived by others as external to that being.
—D.W. Winnicott "Transitional Objects and Transitional Phenomena—
A Study of The First Not-Me Possession"

Trees have been growing in our ribcage to block out sound
I love the way this chair enfolds on we
These trees remind us that there's no places to hide
and that the core of the earth is still the coldest
no matter how much I and I
                      wish the birds could sing for we
every mantle is a mother's broken neck impressed upon by the lattice of the family
and even still, the broken windpipe sounds like a recorder
It's not a woodwind but the sound of brutality bouncing off iron

I/I

      are machine

                          and other machines are history's surrogates
every leaky faucet is symptomatic of a UTI
and the failure of time pushing against a urethral structure
        I am told this is what happens when something gets shoved inside you
        what gets shoved in a sink, still emits discharge

We machine and
technical, gleaming interruptions
others are passengers
vehicle means

transexclusionary signs at pussy marches

by reified TERFs
who openly practice acquired performances of

satanic rites of self-immolating white ghostly supremacy
filled with confusion
by the presence
and
exaltation that one can become many things not purely flesh bound
of gestational and inflatable menstruating tissue
meaning that one's aliveness can be created and co-created
versus
the binary definitions of 18th century definitions providing refuge for bigots
that beg the question:
Would thoust like to suffer miserably
based on how bright one's flesh
burns to an devouring vulgar Saturn?
Where time does not heal
But festers and fetishizes being

Amon Duul's *Between the Eyes*

Time is a border outlined in infinite stops
Which is to say
Is not infinite at all
And is instead a feeble framework for understanding enslavement
Daylight savings time begets bondage
Begets Mississippi purchase begets a need to burn plantations
almost Revolution, predating Paris communes post Grundrisse
Begets prison leasing begets summers of fury begets prisons
Begets this suited lifestyle retail experience
Consumed in the form of creaky knees and sneakers meant to be broken in on the shopping floor
The south can burn again
And it is everywhere

"Volunteered Slavery"

This was never made for consumption
but it was meant to explain
that there is joy on the edge of every knife
illicit unwanted horror
growing underneath aching pleasure
betraying said horror
under a beating molted version of
my hope

skin is exposed   gaping and dripping

Let me fly myself through 19 blocks
until death or distance do we part
there should be an acknowledgment
of such grave digging
from which graves one is not to meant to rise

Aren't we the picture of fragility
a hint of desperation and battery acid
sliding over my tongue
onto yours

You know where to find me
against the slain to the left of
a syncretized San Miguel
at the foot of such an expansive history

Nothing settles harder on the belly
than rocking
back and forth
through obsolescence

I find myself blessed
cloaked away from the
eyes of enemies
and those that wish
to run their razor tongues
against me

Never in the company
of my peers
it's your children
I shall inhabit

Eye Shaking King

Let there be light on a room of
my past mistakes
coated in flesh and lacquer
you're on the outside of
the ambient noise of my joke
looking in

Descending hooves
from under raw hemmed
time is deadstock
in the sea of bleeding future
fountains for containment
purposes

Give me room to scream
there are nothing but
mirrors in this
global spatial triggering
aftermath:
I can title the event from
the gap in my teeth
I just can't
stop it
from creeping up
on me at a traffic light

Our Black Gemini
a good year to mourn
letting the light in the room
catch our skin
you want me pliable
so that my form can be
small enough
to hold your desires
my material form
cannot bend to
the form of a cup
instead I am phallic
a wand
to be beat
over the boss's head

...And The Heavy Loaded Mothers

The African-American male has been *touched,* therefore, by *the mother,* handed by her in ways he cannot escape, and in ways that the white American male is allowed to temporize by a fatherly reprieve...It is the heritage of the mother that the African-American male must regain as an aspect of his own personhood-the power of "yes" to the "female" within.

–Hortense Spillers, "Mama's Baby, Papa's Maybe: An American Grammar Book"

Anterior tilt towards the sun
amoeba tissue paper moons
knowledge of how to hug a corner

My
mistake

I held too close to the sound
of my own heart breaking
and with the residual ill will directed towards your image
I forgot even the meekest of bitches can act
brand new

and   *h o l l l l l l l y w o o o o o d*
Hollyywoooodddd

Under the glaze
there is sludge
under the sheen
there is that poor odorless but feral smell of

21

America
mangled on your tongue
this Moorish Temple of Sistars of Contemplative Desire

To know where I get my tongue from
wrapped in the mystique of black leather and the handiness of becoming phe(male)nomenon
Rilke
all angels are terrifying
that is why when you
walk with me
there is a biblically accurate
eeeeee
        SSense
of intimidation
Darker My Love Grows
smoking time
Freud said, history would have preferred my name was Oberhauer than Freud
ask me again if there is an issue with racial capitalism in the precocious unconscious
when
the fact is
we are inundated with relics
of white insecurity
for all survivors of moksha
as the sinkholes of Philly coalesce

                        to

                                        dentro de

                        exact class war

                        What pro- life ideologues get wrong about proposed

false dichotomy of becoming-being in the body
creating new life

is that it is the symbiotic dance to life
the mother and child co-created

dentro de

winnicottian intersubjectivity of the
hallucinatory fantasies of the womb and child that
dictates the relationship
They are not separate entities but
one being be-coming
The truth
that no one consents to being born

To Here Knows When

John the Baptist lost their
head and strayed from chronos time
they walked in the desert with me
I felt my own voice bounce off my skull
the world is empty but not lost
I'm empty with rot but not full of fatalism
what was there to expect but baptism
but deliverance but happenstance but
companionship
we've all been waiting for deliverance
on an elemental level
hoping to float with grace
in some communal trance
a rupture felt collectively, dripping in blackness soaked by the sun

I leave my mouth open and dry in a half-cracked moan
to share truths on the side of the road

leaning heavy

resentment

the embodiment of a lack of insight

three empty years, full of resentment
in the shape of a slick car

Who has claims when there are no
rights upon future offerings at unspoken hours
an earth wife wants my heart, with open veins into the street
my blood running into the gutter
abolishing futurity

All our dreams came true
and I know our love is true
because god said so on a patented prison made shoelace
we will burn those walls too someday

Soon (with reverb)

Women handling snakes
I wrestle with you
give you my name
display it in my inner lining

I speak
into
your christ wound
growing razors
in my mouth

Borders become   closed
my skin
                              buckles
in between spaces

My capillaries expand as

                              I sew a coat big enough
for our lungs struggling to swell
our class is showing in
the way we wheeze in our sleep
the most impactful autoimmune disease

                              (Asthma)

is not what you think
and could be fixed if our veins
were lined with nickel and copper

and aspirational dreams of
being upwardly mobile

Who loves the air baby?
who can afford these highways when my exchange rate is all the polyps of the Bronx?

who wants the sun baby?

> who can give birth without
> hesitation and advance directives
> for bleeding out on the concrete slab
> and public housing that greets you every morning?

who loves the sun baby when I am the fissure in all social relations and class analysis
alkalizes my teeth to chalk?
who can have the sun baby?
when I can't have you or my memories of us when liberal theories and violent
autotherapy keeps me from you?
lord willing and the flare up don't commence

Paregoric

There's a limp in my voice
that gives out through my knee
I heard someone with the same thing
except it made the sound of wind through a tunnel
of concrete and mortar
and scar tissue
we should all blame the cops for
the influence they have on architecture

Only poor people find rat heads fried in their happy meals
is it a well placed advertisement
speaking to the fatalism capitalism enforces on the
biological meeting commerce meeting sustenance?

All the roads in West Philly are uneven
making my body rattle
shaking as I enter a new atmospheric
understanding of past grudges

There're so many dialects for the hours of night
I should never leave home for nests
and scales

Burning with the fervor of
a choir of my enemies
shaking and rocking their bodies

back and forth
lulling themselves in a chant of
my name

Spent too much time
staring into a
reflection of the sun
that when I looked down
at my stomach I saw
I, and others had been
almost dying
from allergic reactions

Love Theme from Spartacus

However, it must be noted that no one at that time was obsessed with "purity" in regard to race, religion, sex and so on like people are today because that came late in history. People felt in no way inauthentic or hypocritical about having multiple creation stories or adding new goddesses/gods or the like. The reason being that the ancients focused more on abstract lessons and the underlying symbolism of personages than on literal or historical facts. The majority od the modern world simply does not have within its consciousness the possibility of monolatry, henotheism or logic in the form of complementary propositions.
    —Tayannah Lee McQuillar, *Siblys Oraculum: Oracle of The Black Doves of Africa*

Yemaya found me
wandering without
my head

Put me on
a feeling skin
soul spread over you and yours
each belly ache
is a memory of a future

Beneath every basement
is a ceiling
awaiting to be
revived
through collapse

I feel myself recede into my lungs
where I cannot tell you what is wrong
banishing gods from the sky
and bosses from the earth
older than money
crushing commodity fetishes
nominated in the most evil year

Everybody wanna be
made into fetish
talk about being made in the image
2000 years to late
granting you
antiquity
nobody wanna to be of the sea, and forest
everybody wanna be scraps
nobody wanna embrace the deep blackness of earth
shady palm lands
feral sun scorching
pushing against stars and piercing the veil
beyond the night
instead
                    everybody says, "Call me by your slave name"
and I cannot help but to reason
that the only appropriate response is
a punch on the nerve of the jaw
just so you can feel me imbued
with the power of death cudgel of St. Barbara

Driving Me Backwards

Whose violence protected and birthed you?
disaster poetics doing
somersaults off the wall
to be black in love means to unravel and
relive in animation of electrical circuits
recalling a dream, a fermented life
means of recounting bible verses
about how you cannot see to unsee me
Cain is me
I Cain I
can
feel it out in the night,
does my tongue maim known
unknown white supremacists with well intentioned families
with well endowed funds
various liquid funds dry up especially under this climate
blood will rise and soon lay claim
as we twist towards Babylon

Surf's Up
Reciting Latin genus and species backwards
to delouse myself into sleep
Quercus, for all the women in my family
made wooden by life and hard upon touch
Fagus, to bend in the breeze
Prunus,
so that everyone may see me
without sight and my pink aura engulfs the senses

Myself When Young

Anaerobic formations somersaulting into ether
I've gone foraging for other pasts
composting maritime stories
to the down beat of a drum
bleached blotches and histories of storied neglect
topographic desires carved by wind into stones of resistance
no one ever presents their ribs for kicks to overseers and would be landlords
without intentional protracted warfare in mind

Or am I to continue
the Ritual,   getting
racially profiled
in the woo woo shop

Listening to the training of
future practitioners of

              Girlbossing

                    Gaslighting

And mediocre American mindfulness

You are
you (r)
self

    because of the hands that have been laid upon you
      we are selves given unto cosmic crunch
we are all good enough mothers responding to the cry of climate crisis

will it take 5 or 10 years to find an appropriate price for clean air and sunshine rights? will everyone receive a free all-inclusive package to a former commons? Public works becomes defined by the work neededs to keep the public confined within ethnolibertarian borders.

I'll never be able to survive Queequeg's death
conscious grasp of unconscious wishes

A Search for The Reason Why

It was part of the folklore of the slave trade "that a Shark will never follow a Vessel not having on board sick people," but of course they followed most every ship. The greater the mortality and the number of dead bodies going overboard, the greater the crowd of sharks would have been. Observers who wrote of the large numbers of sharks swarming around the vessel were not likely exaggerating. Moreover, the assemblage of hungry predators would have grown when the ship reached American coastal waters, from Virginia south to the Caribbean to Brazil, as the Tiger and Bull Sharks of the western Atlantic would have joined the red wake. Sharks followed the ships in something of a relay.

—Marcus Rediker, "History from below the water line:
Sharks and the Atlantic slave trade"

I should have known when I decided on the muddy path that there would be hooves following after.

Odd-toe family is the name we have given to the Equidae family. Hooved and bathed in the luminous eyes of an inverted black hole. The light dances around them but it is only the blackness of the pupil that provides containment for such marvel. Hippo morphs are the mother of the family, where well-furred rotund beings dwell. Afro. Theirs is the Holy Spirit. Beasts of creation from the land where time began to beat. Eutheria.

UTAN UTAN

Ancient holy god names for manmade disasters for dealing with our obsolescence. Can't you feel it in the air of an unusually warm afternoon? The shift in the patterns of 400 year old sharks who have forgotten their meals, and instead grow fat on the consequences of polluted life?

now die prematurely from natural gas?

we have found the cure for primordial immortality
Agonized Historical Tuesday Mornings
the inflated sense
these mortar hollow baroque buyers of flesh
the main flow of human behavior flows from three
as pleasurable as semen pools in the belly

Two Eves

I am in our garden
listening to you
reading Borges to me
with coin purse present
I am stone
eternally wanting a
life with you
belonging to eternity

In the graves on strangers
Ojalá!
Bring me to hilt
when two gods are in the room
someone must be claimed

You got me *In the Mood For Love*
Hot and bothered over
The question of
"Wouldst thou like to live finally?"

I am that I am

Patron saint of mismatched fingers
Thumb print imprint in the shape of a head

Ark of The Covenant

Come and gaze upon my work
a beauty has come
upon this epitaph is another language   drums beating against the sternum of time
defamation of the Id
a new slur rises

Kirk vs The Family
George vs Parlet vs Brides of Funkenstein
The Congos vs Lee "Scratch" Perry
all things modern in Europe owe a debt to afroasiatic commerce

I am the east coast meteorological goth
The upsetter
Holding critical hope to my chest
There's nothing more attractive than a lack of vision
Up to my ears with jelly specters

A starving poetic pothos
Two-headed oneness
Look within your own house
Before you look
Further
For the origins
Of violence

Illegibility of Pain

Are you afraid of the pain? Or The power?

—Spellling "Queen of Wands"

Pain is something that's understood
and has a thriving political economy.
In reality,
pain   is used by the powerful to
begin the act of dispossession
a barometer of whether
structures
care to understand whether
the wretched of the earth
are actually living at all.
Happiness can't be understood by the capitalist
because they aren't on the side of life.

In the beginning,
is perpetual return
A Beauty Has Come

I swallowed an ember that bloomed in my belly
He's all parking garages on a Tuesday evening when the light goes out
Stacks of holographic memory
Echoing the obsolescence of the dawn of whiteness

I can't use your mandible to orate this feeling
It would require the stretch
On one end, of tongue
And on another, anus

Children screaming at play mimicking the sound of pterodactyls in the future
Covered in feathers
Sipping at water
Speaking of song
Always at play

To be raised in a home of Black skeptics
To look up to the sky
And see your own
Reflection dancing back

The coalescence of the Adirondacks into the shape of geological dreams

Would be leftists

Lust for Life

Spooky action at a distance
île de toi
Isle of you
Eula Mae, I recite your name like a prayer

Everyone is waiting
for me to overrun
and spill
a continuation
spilling over a cup
I'm running off my body
cup
steady bull in the thicket of death at the gate of Ur
let me top you
pronouncing a name as if I am throwing it onto a slab

May 100 machines break and sputter
slouching backwards into Gehenna
face opposite against solid water
every courthouse is an auction block
where I've been in feverish dreams
every burnt out house is an accusation

I am San Miguel
and the devil
casting

fish at the feet
dentro de
    dentro de
        pones tus manos en mi cuerpo

The Sporting Life

But then the white folks started callin' all the slaves together, and for no reason, they started tellin' some of the slaves who their mothers and fathers was, and who they'd been sold to and where. The old folks was so glad to hear where their people went. They made sure we all knew what happened ... you see, they thought it was Judgement Day.

—Amanda Young, oral historian & her granddaughter
Angela Y Walton-Raji on The Leonid Meteor Shower

Finding bits of my hair in
the center of my stomach
even with the star stitched
into my skin
I somehow fall into
the gutter
of another's arms
into other's mailboxes
into another's drafts
thankful not to be picked up
for becoming emotionally disturbed
in a public place
with privatized resentment

My blood vessels are
no longer
sick of me
and have decided to reside inside of me

worth
someone's
desire
a scarecrow of madness
coming alive with Gabriel's horn

There're times when Mercury is stationed direct
and I just feel like my tongue is still tied
my phone is tied up
it won't let me sleep because my sensitivity
has waned and I still can't explain what happened
whether it was an absence of time or my own
leonid shower, where things are
uncovered and covered quickly
like running water over myself
with my clothes still on and understanding
the stains will stay with me
my soul just separated from my body and
that fissure requires time

"Easy 4 U" by Rentboy

Room without light
Room without stillness
The mountaintop strips
Readjusting bra straps
Falling into horse stance
Falling into the shake

Memory 'pon the maritime blues
Of unearthly guesstimation
Pat dry
This cyst won't drain on its on
Memory 'pon the slickness

I wanna make it easy for U
Fill out this definition
A quake under unstable silty earth

People's Republic of Reparations

In the beginning
my beginning
there was St. Peter
at the cornerstone of a Christian tabernacle
1993
nacio de Norte Filadelphia

I was diagnosed with an unspecified cognitive delay
by unlicensed Shepherds of the lord
sticks and stones may have broken dams within
but time has revealed us
a seesaw of death
leaving my four year old
body mute for 24 hrs
keenly aware
a petite awareness

      the lack of peace in a Christian death

      tension begotten
of matter transposes essence
distilled in the rebirth of a hungry ghost

John Rufo reported
in a church
on New Years

under unforgiving light
"The city is named/The land is not"

genetically predetermined to hold shit in
under the surface of skin

humans that once littered the earth with bodies from genocide
continue to do so with sludge, non-biodegradable liquids
and noxious air
until the earth is reborn in our toxic visage

speaking life into an effigy
diversion through the psychoannals of geography
angled moon face

                                                  My obsidian liver
                                                  On this location where I'm from
                                                  We rock Clark's
                                                  Read Marx

Electric voice (Dian Sheng)
Electric Shadow (Dianying)
Hitchcockian Blonde meets Bunelián workers meets Jodowroskyian reality quake
Breathing in
time
Earth's creaking encroachment

"...that lovely place of love that love places for us."

God, I found it.
Under a mountain, months ago, called Salvation.

Something about something about
something aboutSomething
about
something about something about
the yell of them. I hear it in my sleep.

Something
about something
about something aboutSomething
about something about something about
about being cloaked in red, in their eyes.

Something about
something about some
thing aboutSomething
about something about something about
the darkness of ocean and their fearlessness

Something about so…
Something about something
aboutSomething about something about
how they can swim in me, where so many have drowned.

THE BEAUTIFUL ONE HAS
COME
THROUGH
SPACE
NOW
WE CAN BE SATISFIED
IN THE TRUTH
THAT
SPOOKY ACTIONS
AT A DISTANCE
HOLD OUR CENTER
THE BLACK HOLE
NEXT DOOR
SWIRLED INTO A LOOM
TO SEW AND HEW TO A
PREDESTINED PAST
RESIST REVISION
INVITATION TO END ALL KINGS
RESIST ESSENTIALISM
GOODBYE TO FLESH

HUMAN CONSCIOUSNESS
IS NOT THE
METHODOLOGY
EMBRACE TIME
LET ME WITHIN
SWING DOWN SWEET CHARIOT
LET ME RIDE
LET   ME RIDE

We (penetrate) : Nosotros Penetramos

Fingers reaching around skin
It's underneath
it's light
It's a politician
It's the mother-tongue lapping
against a forgotten blown out wall
a pastor asking if I am lonely
he is singing, I see his frustration
wrapping and binding along his skin
isn't negative affinity
a good moisturizer when god
can be counted on fingers and toes
dancing on the tips of pens

Will the Circle Be Unbroken?

Empowered by the rage of a thousand mothers'
A r u m i n a t i n g smell   emits from my glands
        I bleed this month
Garnished with onions this month
Ate green and still e m p t y

                    of envy
Bearing the foresight of a six-sided dream—   *Tago Mago's* bifold
Volunteered slavery resumes in the five days subsequent
prescribing an analysis of the number of ways the indelible markings of love and
biopolitigogical psychic structure
                              "Huh-   ing"
                    into shadow as

the day and hour comes

                    And so
                    They must've
            Raised their hands into the heavens

And cultivated the cosmos
Deep in contemplative desire
The blackness   The darkness
A beauty has come
Breathing in   and

            Out
            of the charcoal, amber and squelching ink of space

Breathe in time

      Breathe out river

Breathe in history

  A Beauty hxs come

      Breathe out revisionism

Breathe in the largest land mass and largest body holding souls within its horn

  A B***** has come

Breathe out the urge to make lineage a brand on the skin

Fat gathers all around protecting organs

to jiggle,   shake and writhing about

to make things juicy and desirable throughout

Cowrie shell sharpened teeth

Deep scratching at the skin

Nights   that pass without days

Love For Sale

Couldn't afford that love
when it was needed
burning everything in my path
except my own Savannah

There wasn't even space for me
in your dreams
gatherin blessings
I cast my affirmations
into a golem of my own creation
the vessel of my body
filled with gypsum

This check running late
the book you were supposed
to commemorate
my reproductive labor is late
my soul
 too
is running late
because
a love life
metabolizing   promissory notes

I hurt before
and will hurt after
There's humming when I wake
everything will continue to hurt
even as the cherry blossoms bloom
even as the magnolia blooms

Cicatriz ESP

Adolescent dreams of body possession
Will clamor and rattle within me?
Or gingerly, but heavy handed,
Press membranes to my walls
And whisper codes
Speaking in tongues about the liberation of Boxcar cadavers

Being introduced to the Cocteau twins because
I said
Chino Moreno's voice
is the most similar to my memory
a heated kiss
First iterations of first contact with the dark one
Mother destroyer
Mother giver
Embody this lust
Spell out the shape for me
Scrye from the pupils all of the details

De eso

Dispose of me
let everyone know
I wanted to explore my wound's veracity

This is a stupid inquiry into a question
I already know the answer to
It's good luck to informally marry me
Many blessings from the madwoman

Miguel

My knee twisted into the
shape of childhood schools
the bone resting
totally popped on the edge of my bed
waiting the storm out
and we just sat filling two cups
caressing fatty pockets
looking for the answer to be no

The aural speculation of plants
by the window both in and out.
Both drowning and not.
Managing their own aliveness
against the sounds
I make when the time of day
Can't catch up, so we made our own

This book cover changes
everyday to match the beating of water
a process better known as sleeping
twined in yew stalks
and making friends with sea creatures
Water was a common theme
A placeholder for wanting to be
in the dark but not too much

Only to know the impossibility of love
making love in the form of a goodbye
A handshake not being ceremonious enough
skin against general sadness not ceremonious enough
negative ions in the air for this ceremony

Spirits Up Above!

In the beginning, I remember there being dust.

Swirling contracting protruding emitting light screeching towards a silent song.

Bones running beneath delta. Flesh beneath stone. Light bending towards echo. In the beginning, a beauty has come. Expropriated during war. Lineage cloaked in falsehoods of nation. Silk rotting behind glass. Prison of memory. The holding of one's things in the afterlife. A holding of the intangible. The beautiful one has come. In the form of noxious air and rememory of warmer valleys. A beauty has come in the preaching of echolalia. In the clamor of war. No war but peoples' war. No war but ending the war on god's favorite: the poor the hungry the lover the upsetters the needy the sun the moon the atmosphere the child beneath sky.

Pushing organs to become new matter. What will I become? Maker, fool, mother or accursed created staring back at creation as the scenery decays for an environment no longer suitable for soft, tender and sensual flesh. When all this points to ecological collapse? The beautiful one has come in the form of blood of my blood in the form of my mind in the form of wish. Decades. Time old wish. The wish to perhaps die but live knowing love and being worthy beyond temporal suffering. I give unto you land that perhaps may not bear fruit, a vinyl collection that contains the compression of the sound of Saturn's rings and milk from my breast if you will have it. Yours is a face I have seen before. In those hours of psychoticism, you have met me. By bodies of water, in the flesh of my lover. One eye brown, one eye blue. The beautiful one has come. I have dreamt of your grasp around my fingers. I know I have not yet lived because I have not found you. I have heard your call in the larks when navy turns powdered blue. In the whistle tone of Xiomara Alfaro. The travel of lyrics 2 go. In the clamor and elbows of Cecil Taylor. I embrace the reverie. I know spring can hang you up the most just the way Betty Carter enunciates the coming of the season. I am all the things I could be because Freud's wife was my mother and then some that is filtered through oceans currents rivers of times reverberating through a kalimba. The beautiful one has come. A warrior born on Sunday.

It'll never be safe to listen to The Beach Boys again.
We all must become
A season unto ourselves
embracing vampiric duties
calling for blood from our lover's shoulder.
(Can you feel/the spirits/
 up above/up above/ up above?)
Can you feel the dense atmospheric misunderstanding call from above?
(Please don't fight the spirit sent from love)
Can you dig the numerous timelines of possibilities that racial capitalism has
interrupted up above?
(Can you feel/the spirits/
up above/up above/ up above?)
Can you feel the limits of intimacy with spirits up above?
(Up above/up above/up above)
Can you feel our flesh bend forth the crunch?

Lorca Drinks A Lime-A-Rita

Tonight, we felt impossibly joyful
no aging bloated men
telling us to stick to the party line
or that we didn't need to know why
Russian workers died for a yet realized state
so many times
and
perhaps it was our generation's fault
and perhaps we weren't vacant in the eyes
in the presence of cowed bedroom'd intellectuals
they all want our youth cum smeared on their lips
exclaiming, "This is where the masses are
but your ends don't match your means
what the fuck is a flash mob?
can I join? does it block the ports?"

Tonight
Comrades   accomplices
fellow travelers
broke glasses in the lenses of
the city
at the ferocity of being ignored
breaking the "rural and urban" false binary
I watched as my arrogance
scattered into the shins of everyone dancing
still music played as red rivers

ached to be more than just rivers, but to be ocean, to be planet
to eventually
                    nothing at all except a still memory

To survive on the nectar of the stars
to crash lovers
this is truly why the capital time clock is a lie

Tonight, I rode out and in
on the waves of dream language
speaking endless tongues
reaching into the back of symptoms
fluffy open symptoms
gifting all the best things that remain free
but require annual check ups
and flunking tests
my throat cracked in two and played a ballad for you
it was scarlet, the color of childhood
rich, on the edge of both life and death
both well and unwell
both well and unwell
you sang to me and said I left lacerations on you
as you were inside
of me

but the term for this event
is reproductive justice
as I cut along months
perfectly etched along a number of life paths
and the unwarranted scaling of mountains

Tonight, I captured numbers without purpose
knowing they would ultimately lose sleep
the breathing and beating automated
illuminating all the years that I fought to
resist from the base of a sebaceous gland
in the vocal cords of someone
who isn't exactly waiting but too loves
to travel and dodges security
while enjoying all god's earthly pleasures
like fainting in the cold and subsequent unrest
She wants me watching, waiting, becoming her daughter
letting the guards know
this marble slab runs thick with our mucous.
It always belonged to us.
And we continue to sleep in
public on public time where
time is slick and watery but coarse when accounted for

Tonight, I kissed you in the dark
letting you know I ultimately failed
and that we are nearing the end
I found a way to sum this all up
without any intervention
No shortcuts. Just desert.

Simon of
The Desert

"I want to get out of this cage
If you want know how it is to be free
If you want know how it is to be free
You got to spend all day in bed with me"
—Rahsaan Roland Kirk "Volunteered Slavery"

"This reconstitution is on the once hand a reparation, a necessary repositioning of the legacy of antiracist struggle for the present that ruptures the hegemonies of gender and class that have scripted the master narrative of the civil rights movement. But the reconstitution of African American literature after 9/11, in addition to sifting through the histories of post-World War II struggles against colonialism and white supremacy to make sense of the present, also turns on the figuration of intimate estrangement from those struggles, the throwing off of civil rights, Black Power, and anticolonial imperatives and the taking up of a tortured fictional poetic engagements with historical figures such as Condoleezza Rice, Barack Obama and Colin Powell and through the depiction of literary characters who bear the weight of post-civil rights anxieties about their agency for state terror after the "successes" of civil rights and the "successes" of a state whose carceral and surveillance apparatuses depend not only on Black objects of scrutiny and discipline but also Black *subjects* of the same.
—Erica R. Edwards, *The Other Side of Terror:
Black Women and the Culture of US Empire*

Azúcar negra

                Sweetback's sweet sweet

                                Badasssss

                                        Black

                                   Dada

                                   Nihilismus

Loooonnnngolsoooong
Sing Swan Song

                  Melancholic orange

Tangerine indigo

Hotbox the foliage
Mason Dixon line rising like the hemline on a mini skirt skimming my thighs
Hangnail moon
Cut down all the trees
And now all there's left
Are haphazard powerlines
To hang water dreams on

Acids rain perforates dreams
The scent of you
Spills through my mind
The gaps in spaces
Filled in
With a Nick Hakim whine

There will come a day when
The holidays
Weeks

Months
Days
That have been hard fought for will no longer suffice.
When the corporate discounts
Promotions,
And appreciation weeks will leave an ashen taste in the mouth

It is identity politics
Until we burn cities
Plantations
Institutions
And whole centuries
Voodoo as a means of conspiracy
Then these magic tricks
Made under night sky
Burning spear dawns
Give new meaning to
"Redistribution of resources"

Reparations is a courtesy cup
That cannot hold the
Drowned water and sweaty tears
That failed to spill
Can you swim?

Feeling vacuum lull
Of alcohol
Sucking towards the
Center of my brain

Open faced chalice
Full of blood
From a series of paper cuts
From the working day
From the pushing back of boundaries hard fought

The hands that leave impression
Pon the mind
Thumbprints impressed
Upon hunger and being
Babbling into mystic rivers of plasma
Material amalgamated
Crystallized into bones, tissues
Connective thought and grandeur feeling

Vellum of unconscious starr'd dream

My mother's waged resemblance to
Chaucer is close but
No banshees' echo mourner's songs

My friends and nem
At the comedy show
Awash in ideological unconscious
That others cannot hold for themselves

Red black green
Spun up in rainbow
Doused in cosmic Blackness

Space and place between sun
Light
Sucking in holding it all together'd

My name in the names of iterations of self
Married to myself,
My love,
Numerous self,
Married to herself,
The Beautiful One Have Come
My name reborn into news limbs
Living by herself

To wait for my body's temperature
To catch up to incubation of disease
Is like watching a child play on swings but instead
Of swings it's like infertility and by infertility
I mean misunderstanding by misunderstanding
I mean collective amnesia by that I mean
"We all lie, and I just decided to go raw with this"

Bitches just want it all
At least this one does

Porque no te quiero

Mira me

Eu som parte

Y

Still, I pronounce it Dixie

They can all die on that mountain

The one surrounded by gates

Rice, sugar cane, children in limbo

Gehenna,

That one

It burns so vividly, with the dying embers

Of the productive labor power of years

With the smell of bottom of the sea in the nose

Everything is running on a slant
Night running within me
Cold pushing me in
How we give such little thought
To the creatures living inside of us

Carrying the night in my mouth
Luring the shadow
Of maidens into the dark
Seeking the perfect song
For failure at an anxious hour

Be honest
If objectification cost this much
You ain't got the money
For it in the first place

Water seeping through electricity
This boxed object will never run again
I only see you when I am mourning
And then it's only when I'm valid
To occupy some bright spot
My pain brings you pain
And that's when you want me around
To make you live
To absolve you of history

Airwells are spaces for one
To breathe in noxious dreams
Never actually big enough for you to feel air

Or to feel really anything
Except the reach of legality, saying
"I care enough for you not to die by my hands"
No one has ownership over the sun
Except of course
If you accept that money
Is the natural order and you deserve
This sunset view with a glass of rosé
When you wake in the morning, and
Your bones don't have to hurt so much
Be grateful that your body didn't have to cram
Itself into the narrative
I love you.
There is almost never a title to the process
That precedes me
Accidentally falling into a spiral
It's not mine to have, but something that was
Given with the stretching of vowels
The breaking of streets
That are meant to crack
When rubbed against the saliva slick rain
It's hot out again
There is a wait period between which job
Which instance I get to call myself lucky
For not dying on anyone else's clock but my own
I need gloves and a suit
To cover the screaming of my blood vessels
So I can say,
"yes, I, too would like to eat and not get headaches from that absence."
The absence that exists both in my energy and bank account

You could feel so much
Better
If you would
Just show me
How to funk
Like you do

Eternity is not of this world

In a different time
Your family used a highway to erase me
To make me sick
To make me write this way
Rich white people want to differentiate
Themselves from poor white people
In the form of hills and elevation
As a way to be closer to god
And away from the fact that Liverpool and Manchester
Only exist due in direct correlation to the
Trans-Atlantic Slave Trade

Juvenile prisons adorn the town like a sickle
The opposite of a blessing moon
When my body sweats against your history in its light
This is the adorning of rust meeting flesh
To accumulate souls in the countryside
Where the love story of capital begins

And to be poor and white is to either
Be a wet nurse to be consumed by whiteness
A maiden to statecraft apparatuses
Or to be race traitor

This distinction is fictitious
Some may say this reads like a funeral
And the answer to this phenomenon is
It is yours, and not mine.
Because funeral is also fictitious
Something created in the pre-war
During and post war which is to say
It is present in this egg and cheese sandwich
It is bellyache, it is wet dry season
It is the reason why I don't call anymore
No, there is no room or air and
The best way to travel publicly is to not.

New York being the place
Where the end time becomes a playground
Burning paper into the shape of a mouth
Mirrors being located on different planes
Mirrors finding their own mirror
The action of being left
Behind in a bloated paper bag
Mirrors selling out
Mirrors being just that
And breaking
The reinvention of exhibition
The spectacle of the white imaginary

I pushed my hand into the dirt
That was your belly
That was tangled cord
And pulled my hand back, away from the church
Away from the loneliness of youth
Away from my verses on stoicism
Instead I am welcoming the sutures
That form the possibilities of union
In the form of garlands of hydrangeas

I'm losing my mind against
The bilevel
Mid-level
Scaffolding
Of anti-Blackness
I am what I am when I am
With you
A play on decolonial pastoral maladies
Tucked in army reserves
Sucking teeth routine tick
Fun surveillance techniques

When there is nothing left
I can no longer suffer for you
Now that I've felt love's length
In my intestines
The courage of being a Black woman in love

If anyone held
The night skin hostage, it would be you
You held the moon too tight
All that remained was dust on your lips
You wanted the depth of ongoing sun beneath snow
Instead, you let your fingers roam the earth
For simplicity, found a cave with what
Resembled light and said "this is love"

You bound me to a rock to sink
I got swept up in Neptune's waves

I wanted depth, I wanted to drink the salt
And have it burn through my veins
I wanted a say in how I'd sink for you,
Instead I was lured into a trap
And had the stars split open under yr knife in my belly
Obscuring the future

Watch my shoulders rack and dissolve
I am only political in the situation
Where I am most audible
Say the Twitter politicians
I am only smoldering sexually
When it is for someone else's use

There was once a ranking on
Which snuff video
Was most popular
Was most deserving
Of sodium, and jelly
Oil paint under the fingertips
But   there's generational violence and not for me to claim
I could teach you   to swallow   like   this   too
This meaning, the stammering of the buckling concrete
The girdling of extended roots of a tree a mistake of mine
Misunderstanding
what is "of" versus "have"
And any other suffix form
The property damage argument made
Me bite my own tongue and bleed

Across time lapsed puddles fixated on its own finality
Infinity always calls home and the bourgeois
Is still young enough to die on history's doorstep

I'm coming for you
I am coming for you all

Now That We've Found Love What Are We Going To Do With It?

Awaken into the ancient songs of prehistoric dinosaurs who all we offer is garbage on Tuesdays and litter on other days. The chittering and hyper gnashing of beaks. Awaken into the flesh of my love. I press our bodies close. Hoping they might fuse. This new body will be composed of hands cradling hearts. Ears listening for breath, dreams and startling awake. Eyes gazing inwards but only briefly to catch the sky. A tail to maintain balance for our flesh home. Always warm with clammy feet. Now that we've found love what will become of our separation anxiety? I feel around the wage incision and make excuses to not press our bodies against each other. Limbs and tails, mandibles and clavicles unlock. The wage incision festers and is a wound that isn't closing. Now that we've found love what are we going to do with the value form?

Primordial new

God don't let me get me bored

In the figure of Moses unto her people

Anointed by the vessel of liberator

On Romare Bearden's Black Circe

Contemplative ache windows gather a venture into the well-worn soul
The pharmakon presents itself after trial and error within earth
Using Daedalus's tongue to make a person out of me
The name translates to the beautiful one has come
A beauty has come in the cosmic stretch of a Betty Carter vowel
The beautiful one has come in the banging of keys against the skulls of tomorrow
Discordant does not mean dishonest or incomprehensible but instead the shape of dissent
Cecil Taylor
A beauty has come
In the cosmic slop
The beautiful one has come to express our discontent and fulfill wish in flesh
The beautiful one translates into broken Canaanite and into Black Athena and Hypnos
Unburdened sleep

Maggot Brain

Our world locks up babies
for killing their abusers
the whole town is mourning
and it finally decided to rain

Schizophrenic skins
is the body a prison
when it's the
most insured material
on earth

Divine separation
I swallowed the blood
and spit upon this obelisk
state capitalism
is when we have to bargain
with money for our souls

In the dusk of rot
in the presence of measurement
I dream of water every night
drowning every night in poison
breathing fire
I've seen it
it's a heat that shakes in the hips
and settles there
maybe offering

a cleansing spell or two
"And how can I help you
if you can't pick up the phone,
walking in the pitch black dark
love in the time of scarcity
love in the time of disease
being gene tagging
It's already attached.
That's the history of flesh:
inaudible cries (y or n)
chance locations(yes/no)
falling apart on the wooden steps of a party
(yesnoitwasafterdinnersoyes)

AND[no] because damn,
I'm that deep, I forgot to get hardened to it
don't ask what it is because
it knows and can answer for itself
and it's always been that way
and it walks around cloaked
in the smell of my moon
the end of all ends
the grand ouroboros
at the bottom of a happy meal

Niggas at the edge of water
at the edge of the end
we already have the sea
Santa Muerte already kissed me

Am I being engulfed
in the flames of hell or
calling upon
the flames of hell from my heart
a name older than drums

The Playlist Remains The Same in The Electric Church

Autumnal desert
an organic resource for metaphors
she could be browned by death
but never black

Everyone's patriarch is in the hospital
except mine
he's stretched against the south
in dirt back road
turning against
taking blood and flesh
into another bastard

Give me a border
And I'll show you Haiti's mountains
And the DR's countryside
In the shape of a meridian along the Atlantic
The house always wins
Across another sea
Caballeros of paler horses of time

Truth of wound
I came up for air at any moment
a lump that grew into a
lip speaking tone death
dripping signifiers
I love the smell of busy
lavender in the night air

Uranus

Icky shame that I've placed into a box beneath a garden bed
I went down into the bed of the lake
Fought against the pressure
Fought against the burning of lung
And esophagus lining
Breaking   open   my rib cage
                              leave space for impossibilities to arise and for future
                                  weapons, shivs and shanks to be formed with care
                        and whispers of evocations etched in marrow

We humbly invite you all
              hope you accept our invitation
To visit the final resting place of the capitalist stakeholders, petty landlords, and those
that wished against life to sustain deadly pleasures of the pockets
                                        We throw dirt upon
                                        the past, we bury your land
                                        deeds, we have no use for
                                        song because we host
                                        a disco right after such an
                                        occasion.
We have no tears to shed, we have been wrung dry.
We have no praises to sing now that our tongues are untied.
We have no caresses to leave the ungrateful dead, because we finally have life and
Let us get on with it and be done.

The Audience With…

The audience with Betty Carter sounds of forever Oakland springs
As if it is comforting that cherry blossoms can coexist and accept forgiveness from
cacti phallgyno curls towards sky
Inside Betty Carter sounds like the top of spring overlooking the horrors of winter to
come before stopping to rest between global warming sunsets
As if I come bearing gifts to Ms. Carter
My heart held outside of my chest as an elusive
"Now it's all in the past"
Slips as she saunters away
An alphabet of fragrance hanging on the wind

The former

                                    Invites
                                    Hold   the bowels
in   hand to offer to the altar of Miss Carter.
You become the   air traveling through her lungs
Made whole   in the white blood cells   that inhabit her
lung capacity
Muscles massaging the urge to scream

My condition my condition my conditioo **O** oonnnnn

                                        ooooooo **O** onnnnnnnn tiioooon

Was
Chronic
Extinguished in the radiation of sonic winnicottian oneness.
      Mother giver
      Mother giver

                        Spring
                        can
                        reallly
                        hannnn
                        nng

Yo. U
Uupppp

            The. Most.

                        tttt.tt.t

Restraint within such a small frame.
Wrapped muscles.

Bird In Hand

Being asked to move into time
To places wishes and daydreams
Into rivets and seams
Being asked to move back into categorical understandings of regrets
In order to fight against disintegration
Carrying a placeholder for liminal s   p   e   c   t   r   u   m   s
Reading somersaults into lecture
Move me, unmove me, place unto y'all's metaphoric understanding the dreams which
have yet
To be realized
Wish unto me, unfurl around, open
Gasp   gasp
                                                        gasp
Cry out, there are ways of understanding that leave indelible marks on membrane surfaces

We should all be so lucky to exist
To not function
The eyes   cease to work
The throat   struggles to open
The ears   seek love remarks
The skin   wrinkles to make space for the grandchildren we wish into the future
Au Revoir, my love: you have my best and my sword to cut through the meat of life.

Hopefully, you have a better grip than me. Hello long love, I seek you out amongst the
fleshy cavernous walls where memory lies.

Food Not Bombs

"Relaxing, partying, learning and teaching and talking about what was happening with Black people all over the world, was a natural tonic. Yeah baby, Revolutionary Cultural Exchange"

–Kuwasi Balagoon, *A Soldier's Story:*
Revolutionary Writings by New Afrikan Anarchist

I find myself in you
Stumbling into places
When you spoke of witch-hunts becoming part of primitive accumulation
The question also begged the present reality of who would be there to take care of children

We all know how to find that Knick of love in a lil knife play
Welling up in the form of bright rubies making space for Bakunin against the state
form and a side of potatoes
Seizing Kropotkin in a quick sandwich
We know how to make due with what's given
We wish to extend this invitation to taste lemonade flavored oceans
With Parsons hidden in the hunt of dill
Of onion based broth dialectical tricks
Balagoon dictating the movements of the body under stress but with the promise of
relief, always

Always that our most vulnerable deserve love and warm sunny places

Return of Saturn

"I'm a cork on the ocean…"
I've searched through the peepholes of space
Through the cosmic brain
Scoured and wrestled through tendrils
Been rocked back and forth
Others have argued my essence is dead
But
all in all,
still very alive
Buried in warm

"How deep is the valley…how deep is the valley?"
Underneath the multitude of orgasms
Felt and unfelt
Between bites of honeydew melon
Within the deep and mucus lined halls of history
Gushing over my jaws, onto my chest
Into your mouth
Spit it back at me
I am not offended

"It kills my soul…"
And in that moment, I swear I almost reached nirvana but was interrupted by two
missed calls

Hello?

Yes?

The way you communicate makes me sick inside?

Hello? Yes?

Okay,
have a
good
one.

With blood still wet on the ground? This is the question you pull from your heart to ask me?

Let the future and past remain unsplit

(Black Sound) A Call And Response

Many blessings for the most high
Kali Ma
Time before time
An exodus from temporality
A loophole into future pasts
Loopholes into the endings of worlds
Exits into new life and vegetation
Sludge   sludge   bile
and the conveyor   belt   of   veins   that   tether   us   to
          umbilical cords of patience
Time
          after
                              time
Time to die to begin to eat to hunger hallucinate the oneness with the mothering breasts

(Black Sound)

Enumerating the spaces between
L   i   g   h   t
Colorways, the gravitational tension   of   space

(Black Sound)

Moby Dick opens with the congregation on a snowy night
Black flock, The Blackness of Darkness
The

(Black Sound)

The spaces between aren't where light is emitted but instead a space for healing and for
Maggot Brain to rip into me

(Black Sound)

The only humans involved must truncate themselves
Cutting
            life here
                                Cutting
attempts at protracted love
Cutting   connections to space time and

(Black Sound)

Haven't you heard
It
,Black poet?
In the sound of scholastic disciplinary actions visited upon children
They don't like Black people

They like

(Black Sound)

The silencing of dissent
Search for The Reason Why
The blackness that holds space and time together
Blackness as congealed time.
Blackness is an invitation to interrogate
Tear asunder, rip it off my body
social relationships holding the fabric of oppression
and resistance

((BlACK

Sou

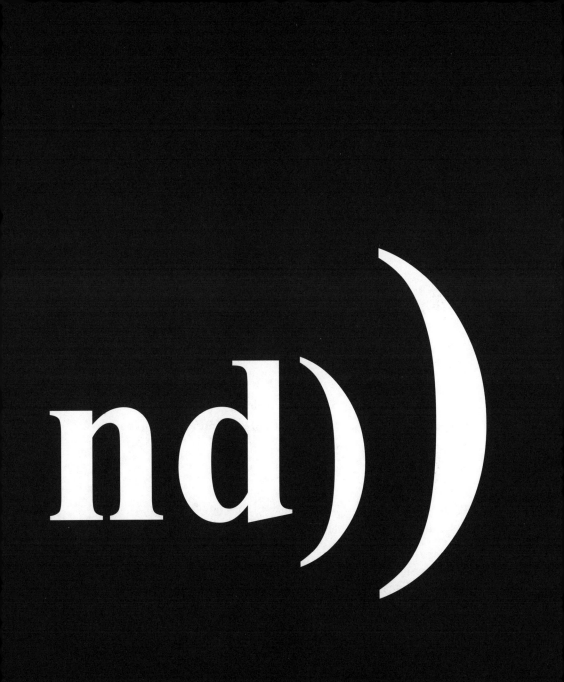

On Can's "Halleluwah"

Parallel procession
Hallelujah and the mythological neuroses don't rise
Spiral Fortitude
What are we going to do now?
Now that we understand that the center of life, a bangle of stars circling this Cosmic
Echo
This blackness
where in life is emitted
there is no escape from this primordial choreography

We've all been dreaming
Of Mother destroyer
Mother giver, of all things unpromising and uncompromising
Destroyer, everything must be accounted for whether light is present or absent
Blackness after all is absolution and the speed of light must reckon its path to
accommodate this expansiveness

Motherfucker, shut up
How many lives do we live for the taste of sunshine and liberation?
What will we do now with our talents?
Do we sell them along with the future or is this message brought to you by a corporate
sponsor guaranteed to rid itself of guilt?
The guilt from knowing the captor is made human at the site of violence visited upon
the captive and not the other way around?

What will we do now when organizations and institutions and states understand that
change is not encompassed by identity reification but instead stamped by liberation?

What will we do now,

Now that we understand that the reading of trees, landscapes, caverns, and pillars has less to do with their existence and more to do with managing our own obsolescence?

I am Eddie Hazel

Here to set your synapses on fire

An electric spirit speaking through

Electric shadow

Moving pon water in the dark

If you hear any noise

It's just me

And the boys

Bundling hope into a burlap funk sack

Mother Earth is pregnant for the 7th time and has decided the birth can no longer be decided and to encourage us to pass on the future enthusiastically or

Be eaten whole after getting caught on the after birth's teeth and grip

Here I stand

Sonically informed

Life is not to simply suffer

But the point is to

Be made   Remade

The practice of reaching an image

"...Love Came My Way..."

Love is apart from all things.

—Jack Gilbert "The Great Fires"

The weight of my love for you is
a plantation on fire
and every financial system
choking on the gravity of reparations

The weight of my love for you is
the antithesis of the result
of pundits fervently insisting
cops exist in the future
when every slave patrol will have its day

The weight of my love for you is
in the twisting of ankles
after storming the gates of Heaven
we all limp into the aftershock of a bender
letting you know to throw down
the irons you found me in
I am nodding off into the oblivion
I wish to reside in

The weight of my love for you is
the failure of the global economy

because it couldn't
enumerate all the tongues
and accents of "joy"
and the nine of cups echoing
"I have everything I want/ I am what I want"
It is our love song, our disco, our sonámbula.

Acknowledgments

Thank you, reader before the reader, John. My frequent collaborator, smile maker, soul influencer, light bringer, colleague, earth wife, distillation of matter that has found me in this time. Thank you.

Thank you, Mommy, Taylor, Mom-Mom +Pop-Pop. I am filled with deep gratitude and pride when I look into each of your faces. You all represent the beauty and strength of all the things you can be as a dope person in this world. You have all guided me and provided bridges of understanding, knowledge and love. Thank you.

Thank you, Laura + David. The love you two share has created the most precious person in my life. You have shared that love and kindness to me, and I am grateful to you both.

Thank you to my community. My own galaxy of superstars (said in an Yves Tumor voice on the song: "Super Stars"). Sophia, Madison, Reek, Ted+Theo+Nella+Wiz, Stephanie, Benedict, Fana, Courtney, Kashif, Anu, Carlos, Amy, Sean, Max, Saralee, Soleil, Christopher, Nila, Chip + Bobby, Wes, Edna, Ed, and many others that have embraced and held me.

Thank you to Nightboat books. Thank you to my midwives Lindsey Boldt, Jaye Elizabeth Elijah, Stephen Motika, Gia Gonzales, Caelan Ernest Nardone, Trisha Low, Lina Bergamini, HR Hegnauer, Kit Schluter, and Megan Tatem who have helped me birth this beauty. Thank you Andrea Abi Karam for your work as a fellow traveler, comrade and indomitable writer. Without you, *Don't Let Them See Me Like This*, wouldn't have reached as many readers. Thank you Ricardo Hernandez for opening your home to me for my first in person reading in three years.

Thank you, Montez Press, Belladonna, Jos Charles for Academy of American Poets, and *A Perfect Vacuum*, and Stacy Szymaszek. Thank you for soliciting and publishing my work that would later become this book.

Thank you Jos Charles, manuel arturo abreu, Hanif Abdurraqib and Chris Nealon for generously offering your words to provide a spell for my work to come into this world.

Thank you to the artists, thinkers, workers, musicians, writers, and my clients that have provided refuge and vulnerable artistic space for me to thrive. Art, theory, and a political insistence on being were never tools that the master owned. Labor is entitled to all it creates. The history of hope, self-determination, and autonomy remain the locomotives of history.

Thank you, reader.

Jasmine Gibson is a Philly jawn, poet and social worker. Her work has been featured or reviewed in *The New Yorker, PoetryNow, Entropy, Hyperallergic, Datableed Zine, LIES: Journal of Materialist Feminism, Poetry Project, The Adroit Journal* and more. She received her B.A. in Political Science from Temple University and M.S.W. from Hunter College, Silberman School of Social Work. She is the author of the chapbooks *Drapetomania* (2015), *Only Shallow* (2020), *BC* (2020), and the full length collection *Don't Let Them See Me Like This* (Nightboat, 2018). She is a student at The Psychoanalytic Center of Philadelphia, training to become a Psychoanalyst.

NIGHTBOAT BOOKS

Nightboat Books, a nonprofit organization, seeks to develop audiences for writers whose work resists convention and transcends boundaries. We publish books rich with poignancy, intelligence, and risk. Please visit nightboat.org to learn about our titles and how you can support our future publications.

The following individuals have supported the publication of this book. We thank them for their generosity and commitment to the mission of Nightboat Books:

Anonymous (4)
Kazim Ali
Abraham Avnisan
Jean C. Ballantyne
The Robert C. Brooks Revocable Trust
Amanda Greenberger
Rachel Lithgow
Anne Marie Macari
Elizabeth Madans
Elizabeth Motika
Thomas Shardlow
Benjamin Taylor
Jerrie Whitfield & Richard Motika

This book is made possible, in part, by grants from the New York City Department of Cultural Affairs in partnership with the City Council and the New York State Council on the Arts Literature Program.